FIGHTING FOR EQUAL RIGHTS

A Creative Minds Biography

FIGHTING FOR EQUAL RIGHTS

A Story about Susan B. Anthony

by Maryann N. Weidt

illustrations by Amanda Sartor

Carolrhoda Books, Inc./Minneapolis

*To my wise women friends, who always find
something useful to do with their lives*   —MNW

Text copyright © 2004 by Maryann N. Weidt
Illustrations copyright © 2004 by Amanda Sartor

This book is available in two editions:
Library binding by Carolrhoda Books, Inc.,
  a division of Lerner Publishing Group
Soft cover by First Avenue Editions,
  an imprint of Lerner Publishing Group
241 First Avenue North
Minneapolis, MN 55401 U.S.A.

Website address: www.lernerbooks.com

Library of Congress Cataloging-in-Publication Data

Weidt, Maryann N.
    Fighting for equal rights : a story about Susan B. Anthony / by Maryann
N. Weidt ; illustrations by Amanda Sartor.
      p. cm. — (A creative minds biography)
    Summary: A biography of one of the foremost women in the battle for
equal rights and the vote for women, Susan B. Anthony.
    Includes bibliographical references.
    ISBN: 1–57505–181–8 (lib. bdg. : alk. paper)
    ISBN: 1–57505–609–7 (pbk. : alk. paper)
    1. Anthony, Susan B. (Susan Brownell), 1820–1906—Juvenile literature.
  2. Feminists—United States—Biography—Juvenile literature.
  3. Suffragists—United States—Biography—Juvenile literature.
  4. Women's rights—United States—History—Juvenile literature.
  5. Women—Suffrage—United States—History—Juvenile literature.
  [1. Anthony, Susan B. (Susan Brownell), 1820–1906. 2. Suffragists.
  3. Women—Biography.] I. Sartor, Amanda, ill. II. Title. III. Series.
  HQ1413.A54W44 2004
  324.6'23'092—dc21 .   2003004130

Table of Contents

1

Do Something Useful

Lucy Anthony hummed a soft lullaby to her baby daughter, Susan. Lucy loved music. She sang whenever her husband, Daniel, wasn't around. Daniel thought music was a waste of time.

Susan Brownell Anthony was the second child born to Lucy and Daniel Anthony. (There would be eight in all.) She was born on February 15, 1820, in a large New England farmhouse that Daniel had built. The sturdy house sat on a hill in the Berkshire Mountains, a mile from Adams, Massachusetts. Behind the house loomed Mount Greylock, the highest mountain in the state.

As Susan grew, she explored the mountains and valleys with her brothers and sisters. Susan's parents let her drag around an old rag doll that she loved, but the family owned few other toys. Daniel thought they were a waste of time, too. The children made up their own games instead.

Susan was happiest playing outdoors. She might spend hours studying an anthill. Or she would watch the sun set behind Mount Greylock. Sometimes Susan liked to sit and daydream. She dreamed that someday she would become a Quaker minister.

Susan's father was a Quaker. Like any religious group, Quakers had their own set of ideas. Most importantly, Quakers believed there was some good in everyone. Music and dancing, they said, could distract a person from finding the goodness inside them. They frowned on toys and games for the same reason. Susan's mother was a Baptist. She never became a Quaker herself, but like most women of her time, she kept quiet about her beliefs. She let Daniel decide how their family lived.

When Quakers gathered to pray, they called it a meeting. At Quaker meeting, everyone sat in silence. From time to time, someone might be moved to speak from the heart.

In the early 1800s, many people didn't think women

should speak in public. Yet at Quaker meeting, both men and women were welcome to speak and pray out loud. Because Quakers believed in the goodness of each person, they felt that men and women were equal, so there was no reason for women not to speak. Susan's grandmother and aunt often preached at Quaker gatherings. Susan grew up feeling that she could speak out, too.

Susan's father was an independent thinker. He didn't do things just because other people thought he should. Daniel, for example, had married Lucy even though other Quakers disapproved.

He refused to pay his taxes because he knew that the federal government could use his tax money to pay for a war. Quakers believed that war was wrong. When the tax collector came, Daniel would put his wallet on the table and say, "I shall not voluntarily pay these taxes. If thee wants to rifle my pocketbook, thee can do so."

Like many other Quakers, Daniel also believed that no one should vote. Voting meant that one side won and the other side lost. Quakers thought that was a bad idea. Instead, they felt folks should talk until everyone agreed. Sometimes that took a long time.

When Susan was three years old, she stayed with her grandparents for six weeks. They read to her every day. Susan loved it. Soon she was reading by herself. She even learned to spell. Every day she read for hours. When Susan came home, her eyes were crossed. Susan's eyesight grew stronger with time, but her left eye remained crossed all her life.

Still, Susan and her family visited her grandparents' house often. She especially liked the little closet under the parlor stairs where Grandmother Anthony kept a tub of maple sugar. While the grown-ups were talking, Susan would hide in the closet and gobble down sugar until her stomach hurt. As she licked sugar off her fingers, she would listen to her father talk about his new cotton mill. The mill took raw cotton and turned it into cotton cloth. No one wanted scratchy homespun linen sheets when they could have soft cotton, Daniel said. He had high hopes for his new business.

Daniel hired teenage women to work at the mill. They worked twelve hours a day, six days a week. Their pay at the end of a week was less than two dollars. That wasn't much, even for the early 1820s, but it was more than they could make working on their families' farms. They also received their meals and a place to live—some of them right in the Anthony home. The Anthonys had as many as eleven boarders at one time.

With all these mouths to feed, the Anthony children were put to work as soon as they were old enough to help. Susan and her mother often baked twenty loaves of bread a day in the large, brick oven beside the fireplace. There was cleaning and laundry to be done, too.

Susan's parents thought everyone should work hard and be helpful to others. They would urge their children, "Try to do something useful with your life."

2

The Worst Girl

Daniel Anthony's cotton mill was very successful. When Susan was six, a businessman in Battenville, New York, asked her father to come and run a mill there. Daniel accepted, and the family packed to move.

Susan's father was in charge of a much larger cotton mill. As the mill's business grew, so did the town. Within ten years, the town had two churches, a post office, a gristmill (for grinding grain into flour), a sawmill, a tavern, two stores, and forty houses. Susan's father built many of the houses for his workers. One of the grandest belonged to the Anthonys. It had fifteen rooms and four fireplaces.

Susan always begged her father to let her work at the mill. Daniel was pleased with her interest in his business, but Lucy didn't think the mill was a good place for children.

Just once, when Susan was about twelve, she had the chance. When a millworker was ill, Lucy agreed to let her daughter work as a spooler for two weeks. Proudly, Susan watched over a loom, quickly replacing the empty spools of cotton thread. For her work, Daniel paid her the regular wage of $1.50 per week. Susan had no trouble deciding what to do with the money. She hurried to the general store and bought her mother six pale blue coffee cups and matching saucers.

While she worked at the mill, Susan noticed that one of the young women knew a lot more about spinning cotton than her male supervisor did. Susan told her father that the woman should be in charge. Daniel believed in the equality of men and women. Still, he told Susan, it would not be right for a woman to be the boss. Susan listened to her father's words. After all, he was her father. But she wasn't sure he was right.

Susan and her brothers and sisters attended the one-room school in Battenville. Girls had to sit in the back of the classroom. Susan didn't think that was fair. When the class began doing long division, the teacher—a man—refused to include Susan in the lesson. Perhaps he thought girls didn't need to know long division.

Susan went home and told her father what had happened. He was furious. He immediately pulled his children out of school and taught them at home. He even added a room onto the house for a classroom. For an hour each night, he used the same classroom to teach the mill girls. He believed everyone should know how to read, write, and spell. Although Daniel had a lot of energy, the teaching soon became too much for him. He hired a teacher named Mary Perkins to take over.

Giving his workers an education was just one way that Daniel treated them well. He also paid them fairly and made sure they had warm beds and plenty of food. In return, Daniel asked them to do something for him. He asked them to sign a pledge saying they would never drink beer, wine, or other kinds of liquor. Susan's parents followed the same rule themselves. They thought drinking was improper. At parties, Susan's mother set out lemonade, tea, and coffee with her fresh doughnuts and gingerbread.

There was no music at the Anthonys' parties, either. Daniel hadn't changed his mind since Susan was a baby. He still thought music was foolish. Mary Perkins thought differently. She wanted to teach music in the classroom, but Daniel said no. That made Susan sad. She liked music.

Music or no music, Susan loved school. She especially loved Mary Perkins. Mary was unlike other teachers of the time. She had her students memorize poems and set aside time for physical exercise. She taught her younger students to read using a book with small, black pictures alongside the words.

With a good teacher like Mary, Susan naturally became a good teacher herself. Starting the summer Susan was fifteen, she tutored some of the neighborhood children. The neighbors thought Susan's father was wrong to make his daughter work. The family didn't need the money, and many people thought it was improper for women to work outside the home. But Susan enjoyed the work, and Daniel believed in being useful. He also believed that women should be able to make money to support themselves.

Daniel was always looking for new and better ways to educate his children. When Susan was seventeen, he took her to Pennsylvania. He had arranged for her to study at a boarding school near the city of Philadelphia called Deborah Moulson's Female Seminary. Susan's older sister, Guelma, was already a student there. Susan had always had a close relationship with her family and had never been so far from home. When her father left, Susan was so sad she couldn't say good-bye.

To ease her homesickness, Susan wrote long letters home. But at Miss Moulson's, writing a letter was no simple task. Miss Moulson was hard to please. First Susan wrote the words on a slate. Then Miss Moulson checked the spelling and grammar. After she corrected any mistakes, Susan used a quill pen to copy the letter onto paper. Then her teacher checked it again. Susan often forgot to dot her i's. (She had a lot to say, and she was always in a hurry.) Finally, five or six days later, Susan mailed the letter. In addition to his other jobs, Susan's father ran the post office, so the family didn't have to pay for stamps!

At Miss Moulson's, Susan studied arithmetic, algebra, literature, chemistry, philosophy, physiology, astronomy, and bookkeeping. Susan was a good student, but she hated reading aloud in class. She didn't like the way she looked with her crossed eye, and her poor eyesight sometimes made her stumble over the words.

Susan felt bad about herself, and Miss Moulson made her feel even worse. Every Sunday after church, the teacher quizzed Susan and the other girls about the sermon. Some of the girls simply received a scolding if they got a question wrong. When Susan didn't know an answer, Miss Moulson would tell her that God would strike her dead if she didn't pay closer attention. The teacher also criticized Susan often for laughing out loud with her friends.

Susan never forgot one experience with Miss Moulson. Susan was standing on her teacher's desk, cleaning cobwebs from the ceiling, when she slipped and broke a lock on a drawer. Right away, Susan said that she was sorry. But Miss Moulson would not accept her apology. She made Susan stand in the corner and think about her "wickedness." Susan told a friend, "Sometimes I feel as if I were the worst girl of all being."

Susan once complained to Miss Moulson that Guelma was never scolded. Miss Moulson said, "Guelma does the best she is capable of. Thou hast greater abilities and I demand of thee the best of thy capacity."

Despite her problems with Miss Moulson, Susan enjoyed her studies. But she didn't even have the chance to finish the school year. In April 1838, her father wrote to say that Susan and Guelma had to leave. He had run out of money, and he was not alone. Everyone in the country was short of money. Sadly, the girls packed their things and returned home.

Business was so poor that Daniel had to close down the mill. To buy food, the family sold everything they owned. They sold the children's schoolbooks, Daniel and Lucy's eyeglasses, even Susan's underwear.

Luckily, Susan's uncle bought the family's favorite things and returned the items to them.

On a cold, windy day in March of 1839, Susan moved with her family to the town of Hardscrabble, New York. They rented a house that had been built as a tavern and hotel. It still had a spacious ballroom in the attic.

One day the young people of the town asked Daniel if they might hold dances in the attic. Being a good Quaker who disapproved of dancing, he said no. But they didn't give up. They explained that if they couldn't use the attic, they would have to hold their dances in a tavern, where liquor was sold. Finally, Daniel gave in. He thought liquor was more dangerous than dancing. All winter long, the young people danced in the attic. Susan and two of her sisters sat along the wall and watched. Susan would have loved to join the fun.

The young dancers were not the only strangers welcomed at the Anthony home. Since the house had once been a hotel, travelers were used to stopping there to spend the night. Some of the visitors didn't realize that the building was now a family home. Luckily for them, the Anthonys were kind-hearted people who never turned anyone away. Besides, they could use the money.

Often there were as many as twenty guests for supper. Once again, Susan baked bread, changed bedding, and cleaned rooms. In her free time, Susan enjoyed quilting bees and sleigh rides.

In May 1839, she left home again. To help with the family finances, Susan had found a job as assistant teacher at Eunice Kenyon's Friends' Seminary, a Quaker boarding school in New Rochelle, New York. Miss Kenyon was often ill, so Susan was usually in charge of all the students.

In the fall, Susan returned home for her sister Guelma's wedding. At twenty years old, Susan was the age when most young women married. She had received several marriage proposals. But she had turned them all down. If she were to marry, everything she owned would become her husband's. He would make all the decisions, and she would have no say. Susan simply was not willing to give up her freedom.

Susan approved of Guelma's new husband, Aaron. Unlike many husbands at that time, he treated Guelma kindly and gently. Yet he still thought a woman's place was in the kitchen. Once when Susan baked a tasty pan of cream biscuits, Aaron told her, "I'd rather see a woman make biscuits like these than solve the knottiest problem in algebra." Susan replied, "There is no reason why she should not be able to do both."

3

A New Friend

In 1845, Susan's parents bought a thirty-two acre farm near Rochester, New York. Susan stayed on the farm for a while, but in the spring of 1846, she went off on her own again. She hated leaving the cherry trees and the peach and apple orchards her father had planted. Still, Susan was twenty-six, and she wanted to be independent. She traveled down the Hudson River by canal boat to a new job at the Canajoharie Academy, in Canajoharie, New York.

Susan became the head of the girls' department. She taught reading, spelling, writing, math, science, philosophy, and history. Susan's wages totaled $110 a year. This time she did not send the money home to her family. For the first time in her life, she bought herself some new clothes. Her favorite purchase was a white straw hat with a pink satin ribbon.

Teaching was hard work for Susan, so she made sure she had time for fun. She got all dressed up and went to the circus. She also attended a dance with a young man. (She might not have told her father about that.)

During her first year in Canajoharie, Susan began to think more about the world around her. Her parents' views about drinking led her to attend meetings of a group called the Daughters of Temperance. The temperance movement focused on helping families. When men drank too much liquor, they often beat their wives and children. To make life safer for women and children, the group wanted to make liquor illegal.

Susan gave her first public speech on March 2, 1849, at a supper given by the Daughters of Temperance. Some people thought it was wrong for a woman to give a speech in front of men. But that didn't bother Susan. After all, her aunts and grandmother had always spoken at Quaker meeting.

Susan had written out her speech and sewn the pages together inside a blue cover. She felt proud as she looked around the room, decorated with red flannel and cedar boughs. On one wall, large letters made of the green branches spelled out her name: Susan B. Anthony. She told the group of two hundred townspeople about the goals of the Daughters of Temperance. She urged women to stop serving wine and other kinds of liquor in their homes.

With her involvement in the temperance movement, her job, and her friends, twenty-six-year-old Susan enjoyed being busy and independent. Still, she missed her family and looked forward to her visits home.

During one such visit in August of 1849, Susan found out that her mother, father, and sister Mary had attended a women's rights convention in Rochester. They had listened with interest to heated arguments for and against women's right to vote. Susan wasn't surprised that they would find such a gathering interesting. However, she teased her father that he was "getting ahead of the times." (Besides, he didn't even vote himself!) Susan's family told her about the energetic team of Elizabeth Cady Stanton and Lucretia Mott. The two women had organized the convention and gave emotional speeches about women's equality. Susan felt her family's excitement. She couldn't help but be curious.

That fall Susan returned to her teaching job in Canajoharie. When she wasn't working, she helped her cousin Margaret, who suffered from painful headaches. When Margaret died in childbirth a short time later, Susan was heartbroken.

With her dear friend gone, Susan found that her life in Canajoharie no longer interested her. She was bored being a teacher, but she didn't know what else to do. Finally, Susan decided to quit her job and go home to her parents' farm. She spent her days picking peaches. She wove rugs out of old rags. She sewed shirts for her father and brothers. At night, she read poetry and thought about what she could do with her life that might be useful.

On Sunday afternoons, many of Lucy and Daniel's friends gathered at the farm. They talked a lot about temperance, women's rights, and ending slavery. Susan loved hearing the booming voice of Frederick Douglass tell about the Underground Railroad. Frederick was a former slave who used his home in Rochester to hide runaway slaves and help them escape to freedom in Canada. Susan wanted to hear every word. But she also loved to cook. She usually ended up dashing back and forth between the kitchen and the parlor.

In 1851, Susan traveled to Seneca Falls, New York, to attend a series of antislavery meetings. There, on May 13, she met Elizabeth Cady Stanton. Susan and Elizabeth liked each other immediately. Susan listened closely as her new friend talked of unfair laws that let men take the money women earned. Elizabeth said that in order to change the laws, women must be able to vote.

She argued that fashion was unfair, too. Tight underclothes and long skirts kept women from doing the same activities men enjoyed. Elizabeth chose to wear a new kind of dress invented by her cousin, Elizabeth Smith Miller. It was loose-fitting and had a knee-length skirt with long pants underneath.

Susan wasn't sure about this new style of dress. She wasn't sure women should have the right to vote, either. But she was fascinated with this woman who was a wife and mother as well as a pioneer for women's rights.

Meanwhile, Susan continued her work with the Daughters of Temperance. She gathered signatures for a petition to ban the sale and making of liquor. The Daughters of Temperance hoped the petition would convince New York lawmakers to pass a new law. The group held suppers and festivals to raise money and spread their message.

Soon Susan began writing temperance articles for *The Lily,* the first woman-owned newspaper in the United States. The paper's owner and editor was Amelia Bloomer, and she focused the paper on issues affecting women.

In the newspaper, Amelia praised Elizabeth Miller's new clothing style so regularly that people began to call it a bloomer dress. Amelia introduced Susan to other women who were working for political and social change. Some of them were abolitionists, people who wanted to ban slavery. Others were suffragists, people who wanted to give women suffrage (the right to vote).

In January of 1852, Susan and several other women were invited to the Sons of Temperance Convention in Rochester. The Sons of Temperance was an all-male group, just as the Daughters of Temperance was an organization of women. The two groups worked together from time to time.

Susan was excited about taking part in the convention. However, when she stood up to speak, one of the leaders told her to sit down. "The sisters were not invited here to speak, but to listen and to learn," he said.

Susan stomped angrily out of the hall. Other women walked out, too. The women found a room in the Hudson Street Presbyterian Church and held their own meeting. Since the night was snowy and cold, not many people attended. Those who were there expressed their frustration with the old-fashioned ways of the Sons and Daughters of Temperance. Susan and the other women made plans to hold their own temperance convention. Susan volunteered to be in charge. She arranged for her friend Elizabeth to be the main speaker.

The first Women's State Temperance Convention took place on April 20, 1852, in Rochester, New York. The group formed the Women's State Temperance Society and elected Elizabeth president. Susan served as secretary. Like the Daughters of Temperance, the group wanted to change people's minds about drinking. They believed not only that women needed this protection but that they deserved to be treated kindly and respectfully.

Elizabeth had an even better idea. Standing on stage wearing short hair and a bloomer dress, she suggested that the state of New York pass a law allowing a wife to divorce her husband for drinking too much. When Elizabeth was finished, Susan cheered. Not everyone did. Some of the women thought Elizabeth had gone too far. At the time, people didn't talk openly about divorce. And the convention was supposed to be about temperance, not about women's rights. Still, the convention gave Elizabeth, Susan, and other women's rights workers new energy to fuel their work.

A few months later, the Men's State Temperance Society held a convention in Syracuse, New York. Elizabeth had recently given birth to her fifth child, so Susan went with her friend Amelia Bloomer instead. Both women sported short haircuts and bloomer outfits. Susan tried to speak but was shouted down. Once again, the women were welcome only if they didn't talk. As much as Susan cared about the temperance movement, she realized suddenly that there was a more important issue that needed her attention. At the age of thirty-two, Susan knew what she could do with her life that might be useful: she would work for women's rights.

In September of 1852, Susan attended her first women's rights convention in Syracuse. She was impressed by the important women she met: Dr. Harriot Hunt, one of the first female physicians; Clarina Nichols, editor of Vermont's *Windham County Democrat;* and Antoinette Brown, the first woman ordained as a minister. However, Susan had to admit that she was also delighted to meet Elizabeth Smith Miller, the inventor of the bloomer outfit.

At the convention, Susan read a speech that Elizabeth Cady Stanton had written. Elizabeth was a good speechwriter, and Susan was a good speaker, so they made a great team—especially at times like these, when Elizabeth had to stay home with her children. In the speech, Susan argued that colleges should be forced to admit women as students. She also said that women should take a stand and withdraw from churches that did not treat them as equals.

The *Syracuse Journal* reported, "Miss Anthony has a capital voice." But the *Syracuse Star* made fun of the gathering, calling it "the Tomfoolery convention." In spite of the criticism, Susan was full of hope. With so many smart women working together, they couldn't fail.

4

Susan Hits the Road

In the spring of 1853, Susan traveled all over the state of New York, organizing women's temperance groups. However, her message had changed a little. She still urged men to quit drinking. But she also told women to leave their drunken husbands. She said, "We are beginning to know that the life and happiness of a woman is of equal value with that of a man." Susan met with men's temperance groups, too. However, many men still felt that women did not belong there.

In June of 1853, Susan and Elizabeth organized the second annual Women's State Temperance

Convention in Rochester. This convention was different from the first. This time, many women spoke up right away about the purpose of the meeting. They wanted the group to focus on temperance, not women's rights—and especially not women's suffrage. They also wanted to allow men to attend. The members voted for someone else to replace Elizabeth as president. Susan was so angry that she quit her position as secretary.

Susan felt defeated. She wrote to Elizabeth and told her so. Elizabeth wrote back and told her friend to forget about the Women's State Temperance Society. "We have other and bigger fish to fry," she said. There were many other people who would welcome their message about equal rights.

Susan took Elizabeth's words to heart. By the next summer, she was again traveling throughout the state of New York. To her dismay, she found that the temperance groups she had helped to organize were all dead. Why? Because women did not have their own money to rent meeting halls or print advertisements. Married women had no legal right to any money they earned. Susan knew that the only way the unfair laws would change was if women had the right to vote. This made her more determined to work for women's rights. So she got busy.

Susan found sixty women to help her circulate petitions around New York State. One petition called for the expansion of the Married Women's Property Act. The petition stated that women should be allowed to keep any money they earned or inherited. The other petition called for women's right to vote. Susan knew that without the vote, women could never improve their lives.

More than four thousand people signed each petition. Susan presented them to New York's state lawmakers. The men replied that women didn't need to have their own money. They certainly didn't need to vote. After all, men took very good care of women. Didn't women always get the best seats in a carriage and the tastiest bits of food at the table?

Susan was angry when she heard what the men had said. She fought back in the only way she could—she hit the road to talk to people about the importance of equal property rights for women. On Christmas Day, 1854, Susan said good-bye to her parents. She took her black alligator bag full of pamphlets and fifty dollars that a friend had loaned her, and off she went. She wished that Elizabeth could go with her, but she had to stay home and take care of her growing family.

Being on the road wasn't easy, especially in the wintertime. The roads were bumpy and snowpacked.

The inns where Susan stayed had no heat. Most mornings, she had to break the ice in the pitcher of water before she could wash her face. Still, Susan preferred winter travel. In the colder months, women were not as busy with gardening and other outdoor chores, so they were more likely to come to a meeting.

When Susan arrived in a town or village, her first job was to find a meeting place. If the minister would not allow her to speak in the church, she tried the schoolhouse. Other times, she made do with someone's living room.

Usually, Susan planned an afternoon meeting just for women. She asked them about their concerns and told them about her petition for equal property rights. Then she invited them to return in the evening with their husbands. It was the men, after all, who could vote to change the laws. Many women—and some men—believed in what Susan was saying about women's rights and the right to vote. Others came to hear her because it was so unusual to hear a woman speak in public. Susan charged each person twenty-five cents to attend. She used the money to pay for her transportation and lodging. Still, Susan often had to take money out of her savings to pay for her expenses. But she didn't mind. She was doing something useful with her life.

Susan worked hard traveling from town to town. She often had to trudge through deep snow in uncomfortable boots, and her feet and back began to suffer. At one stop, she had to be carried in and out of the meeting because her back hurt so badly. Still, Susan insisted on giving her speech.

When she returned home in May of 1855, she told her parents about her trip. She showed them her account book. She had spent $2,291. She had collected $2,367. Susan had spoken and delivered petitions in fifty-four of the sixty counties in New York State. For her effort, she had earned $76—and a sore back.

Susan was becoming well known around the country for her hard work, powerful speeches, and strong beliefs in the rights of all people—not only women but slaves and free African Americans as well. In 1856, Susan was asked to head the New York State branch of the American Anti-Slavery Society. This meant more traveling. But it also meant she would be paid for her work. She wouldn't have to use up her own savings in order to work for a good cause.

Susan's new job did not keep her from working for women's rights. By now, Susan almost enjoyed giving speeches. Still, Elizabeth was better at writing them. Elizabeth wrote to Susan and invited her to visit. She said she would write speeches if Susan would "hold the baby and make the puddings." Susan traveled from Rochester to Elizabeth's house in Seneca Falls, New York. She did more than just hold the baby. She helped out wherever she could. She even punished the older children when she thought they needed it.

In the summer of 1857, Susan attended the New York State Teachers' Convention. She brought along a resolution stating that all schools, colleges, and universities open their doors to women. The members voted to decide whether the group would support this idea. Despite Susan's passionate speeches—which Elizabeth had written—the teachers voted against the resolution. Later, Susan wrote to Elizabeth that she felt discouraged and alone.

Susan didn't stay sad for long. There was work to be done, and she was soon back on the job. In Albany, state lawmakers would finally be voting on the expanded Married Women's Property Act. The petitions Susan had gathered four years earlier helped. In March of 1860, the New York legislature passed the expanded act. Women could sign their own business agreements. They could control their own money and property. They could sue and be sued in a court of law and share custody of their children after a divorce. Passage of this act was a major victory for women.

Susan celebrated what seemed to be another victory in November of 1860: Abraham Lincoln was elected president of the United States. Susan was happy because the new president thought slavery was wrong. Unfortunately, ending slavery was not that easy. President Lincoln believed states that allowed slavery had to vote to change the law. Not everyone wanted slaves to be free. Around the country, people argued angrily.

As head of the state branch of the American Anti-Slavery Society, Susan had her work cut out for her. She organized a team of the finest speakers she knew. Among them were Lucretia Mott, a Quaker minister and an agent of the Underground Railroad; Stephen Foster, a hard-working abolitionist; and of course her good friend Elizabeth. During the winter of 1861, the group toured upstate New York. They carried banners with the slogan "No Compromise with Slave Holders."

The speakers didn't have an easy time. Many people blamed abolitionists for the country's problems. In Utica, New York, Susan was locked out of the hall where she was scheduled to speak. She had already paid sixty dollars to rent it. In Rochester, angry people yelled at Elizabeth until she was forced to leave the stage.

By April of 1861, the country was in an uproar. Armies of the South were fighting against armies of the North. The Civil War had begun. Many of Susan's friends set aside their women's rights work. Even Elizabeth believed it was best to cancel all public meetings on the subject until the war was over. Susan cared deeply about freedom for the slaves. Still, she worried that if they let up on their efforts, the women's movement would slide backward. She was right. In 1862, the New York legislature took out the part of the Married Women's Property Act that gave women equal custody of their children.

Susan felt crushed. She needed a rest. She went home to her parents' farm. She tried sewing and quilting, but these tasks seemed useless and boring. Susan was used to being active. She couldn't sit still. She varnished the library bookcase and washed every window in the house. She also helped hide runaway slaves as part of the Underground Railroad. It wasn't long before Susan tired of housework. She wanted to do something more useful.

In 1863, President Lincoln signed the Emancipation Proclamation. This freed some slaves but not all of them. That wasn't good enough for Susan. The forty-three-year-old moved to New York City, where Elizabeth now lived with her family. The two women set up an office to distribute petitions throughout the country to free all the slaves. They had little money, so Susan walked all over the city rather than pay to ride the streetcar. She spent only ten cents a day for lunch. The women gathered nearly 400,000 signatures. Everyone who signed a petition was asked to donate one cent. This helped pay office costs. Still, the donations weren't quite enough. Susan paid for the rest with her own money. Although it may have been difficult for her to set aside the issue of women's rights, she was just as devoted to ending slavery.

On February 9, 1864, the bundles of petitions were carried in to the Senate. They made an impressive sight. The senators could see that people wanted an end to all slavery. They voted to add a Thirteenth Amendment to the Constitution. Owning slaves was now against the law. Elizabeth and Susan closed their office with a feeling of satisfaction.

After the war, Susan returned to the cause of women's rights. She started her own newspaper. She called it *The Revolution.* The first issue appeared on January 8, 1868. The paper's motto was "Men, their rights and nothing more; women, their rights and nothing less." If a woman became postmistress in Colorado, the item appeared in Susan's paper.

Women writers contributed poems and stories. Susan made sure all the work on the paper was done by women, including the typesetting—a job that was almost always done by men.

Of course, Susan used *The Revolution* to air her own beliefs. One headline read: "ALL WISE WOMEN WILL OPPOSE THE FIFTEENTH AMENDMENT." The Fifteenth Amendment said that everyone could vote, regardless of race, but it only applied to men. The amendment was meant to give black men the right to vote. But what about black women—all women, for that matter? Susan asked. She wanted an amendment that really would allow everyone to vote.

The Fifteenth Amendment passed in 1870. Many abolitionists felt their work was done—slavery was now illegal, and black men could vote. The women's rights movement had always depended on abolitionists to help their cause. Without their support, women were on their own.

5

I've Gone and Done It

In the spring of 1870, Susan published the final issue of *The Revolution.* Printing costs were high, and the newspaper was losing money. That meant Susan was losing money. Piles of bills littered her desk. When she added them up, the total came to over $10,000. Susan spent the next seven years paying off the debt.

Susan turned her attention to a new organization that she and Elizabeth had formed. They called it the National Woman Suffrage Association. Although the organization would allow men to be members, only women could hold leadership positions.

The main goal of the NWSA would be to make law-makers pass an amendment to the Constitution giving women equal voting rights. To do this, Susan began to take a closer look at the Fourteenth and Fifteenth amendments. Perhaps they would be able to help the cause of woman suffrage after all. The Fourteenth Amendment said that a citizen was anyone born in the United States. If a woman was born in the United States, she was a citizen, Susan reasoned. Besides giving black men the right to vote, the Fifteenth Amendment stated that citizens could vote. It made sense, Susan said, that if women were citizens, they should be able to vote.

So on November 1, 1872, Susan did something no woman in the state of New York had ever done: she registered to vote. Her three sisters did, too. Registration headquarters in Rochester was the town barbershop. For a woman to walk into a barbershop was unusual, and the men turned to stare. But when Susan said she wished to register to vote, their jaws dropped. When they could speak again, they said they wouldn't stand for it. Susan talked and talked. She convinced them that they wouldn't get into trouble. Susan and her sisters wrote their names and addresses in a book and signed the forms to show that they planned to vote in the upcoming election.

Four days later, Susan marched to the voting booth. She cast her ballot for Ulysses S. Grant and the Republican Party, because they had promised they would listen to women's demands. This was more than other politicians had promised. Susan wrote to Elizabeth, "Well I have been & gone & done it!" Susan's action made headlines in newspapers across the country.

Three weeks later, a United States marshal appeared at Susan's door. He had come to arrest her for voting. Susan asked him to handcuff her as he would any man under arrest, but he refused. They rode the streetcar downtown. When the conductor tried to collect Susan's fare, she pointed to the marshal and said in a loud voice, "He'll pay my fare. I'm traveling at the expense of the federal government."

Susan's trial began on June 17, 1873. The judge, who opposed women's suffrage, had written his decision even before the trial began. He simply ordered the jury—all men—to find Susan guilty. He sentenced her to pay a $100 fine. Then the judge made a mistake. He asked Susan if she had anything to say. She certainly did. Among other things, she said, "I shall never pay a penny of your unjust fine." She never did, and the judge took no further action against her.

Susan wasn't the first woman to vote illegally, just the most famous. Between 1868 and 1872, over 150 women around the country had tried to register and vote. Women went to the courts. They argued with state officials. In every state, the courts ruled against them.

Susan continued to campaign for women's suffrage. She and Elizabeth traveled across the country with a petition that demanded a new amendment to the Constitution. A senator from California presented the so-called Anthony Amendment to Congress. It failed to get enough votes.

In 1876, the United States celebrated one hundred years of freedom from British rule. The city of Philadelphia held a celebration that included a reading of the Declaration of Independence. This document talked about the rights of all men. Elizabeth and Susan asked if they could read the Declaration of Rights for Women at the same event. The women's declaration outlined the rights the women were fighting for, especially the right to vote. The organizers of the gathering would not let them take the stage, but Susan went to the event anyway. She handed out copies of the Declaration of Rights for Women and talked to people in the crowd about women's rights.

Later that same year, Susan and Elizabeth sat down

to write a history of the women's movement. They worked at a large desk in Elizabeth's home. Each had her own pen, ink, and glue. Piles of letters and clippings covered the desk and the floor around them.

Susan wanted other women to know how hard they had all worked for women's rights. But writing a book about the women's movement proved harder than living it. Susan hated it. She didn't like to sit still. She wrote to a friend that the work made her feel "growly."

Susan and Elizabeth soon realized that they would need help to write the book. They enlisted two other women to help them. The first volume of *The History of Woman Suffrage* was published in 1881. It was 878 pages long, and it covered the history of the women's movement up until the Civil War. The second volume was published in 1882, and a third volume appeared in 1886, almost ten years after they began the project. When the books were finally in print, Susan sent copies to every library in the country. Other women added to the project until the book was six volumes long and nearly six thousand pages.

6

Failure Is Impossible

Susan continued to make history, not only in America but throughout the world. In 1888, she organized an international conference of women. The event marked the fortieth anniversary of the first women's conference in Seneca Falls in 1848. On March 25, women from Norway, England, France, Denmark, Finland, India, and Canada gathered at Albaugh's Opera House, in Washington, D.C. Susan wrote and asked President Grover Cleveland if the women might visit him while they were in the city. The president did not support the women's movement, but he and his wife held a reception for them anyway. No doubt Susan tried to change his mind about women's suffrage.

When the convention was over, Susan knew it was time to get back on the road. The United States was growing, and Susan was determined that new states enter the Union as woman-suffrage states. Other women who were involved in the women's movement felt the same way. In February 1890, Susan and Elizabeth's National Woman Suffrage Association joined together with another organization, the American Woman Suffrage Association. Members of both groups hoped that the new National American Woman Suffrage Association (NAWSA) would be able to do more good than the two smaller organizations had been able to do by themselves. Elizabeth was named president, with Susan as vice president. (Two years later, Susan would take over the presidency.)

Meanwhile, South Dakota was about to declare statehood. So in the summer of 1890, Susan headed west. A young woman named Carrie Chapman Catt traveled with her. Carrie was one of several young suffragists who admired Susan. Susan's role was similar to that of a favorite aunt—in fact, she called the women her nieces. Although Susan still had plenty of energy for a seventy-year-old, it was good to have help.

The two women worked hard. Sometimes they rode for fifty miles in an open wagon to talk to women about their rights. They urged these women to get their husbands to vote for women's suffrage. Susan and Carrie spent many a night in a sod house, as guests of prairie families. Susan admired the brave women who lived in these houses and cooked meals over fires made with buffalo chips. Who could deny them the right to vote?

Sadly, Susan and Carrie's hard work wasn't enough. The women of South Dakota did not win the right to vote. But there was better news in Colorado. In 1893, men in Colorado voted for women to have the right to vote. They followed voters in Wyoming, the first area to give women full voting rights.

Susan was happy for the victory in Colorado. Still, she worried about her home state of New York. So she set out once again. In 1894, the seventy-four-year-old traveled to all sixty counties in New York State. She lectured women—and men, if they would listen—on the importance of women's right to vote. But to her disappointment, New York's lawmakers again voted down the women's suffrage amendment.

Next, Susan headed west to Kansas, hoping to sway lawmakers there. But the suffrage amendment lost in Kansas, too. Did Susan give up? Of course not.

In 1896, she traveled to California. There she often gave three speeches a day. The seventy-six-year-old could talk to anyone anywhere. She would pull a speech out of her black alligator bag and start talking. She spoke at picnics. She lectured in schoolhouses. After a while, she wasn't even surprised to find "Welcome Susan B. Anthony" written on the blackboards of the pool halls. During her visit to California, Susan decided to take a break. She bought herself a bloomer outfit (she had gone back to wearing full-length dresses long before) and rode a mule through Yosemite Valley just for fun.

The women of California liked what Susan had to say. Rich and poor alike supported her. Wealthy women gave hundreds of dollars. Women who sewed or washed clothes for a living gave twenty-five cents a week. Some women went without a new winter coat in order to support Susan and women's rights. Anyone who gave two dollars received a photograph of Susan.

Susan raised more money for women's rights in California than she ever had before. But the Liquor Dealers' League had even more money. They focused on the men—especially in San Francisco. They said that if women got the vote, they would outlaw liquor. Despite Susan's efforts, the men of California were not ready to give up their liquor or to share the voting booth with women.

While Susan was in California, she spent time with a young journalist named Ida Husted Harper. When Susan was ready to return home to Rochester, New York, Susan asked Ida to come and stay with her. Susan had seen women's lives change in her lifetime, and she knew that what she had accomplished for women's rights was important. She hired Ida to write her biography. Two volumes of the book were published in 1898.

By 1900, Elizabeth was in poor health, and Susan was slowing down as well. It was time to let a younger woman lead the suffrage group. Susan announced that she would step down as president of the National American Woman Suffrage Association. At the final session of the group's annual convention, Susan saw to it that forty-one-year-old Carrie Chapman Catt was elected president. With the lights making her silvery white hair look like a halo, Susan presented her friend Carrie to the convention. The women cheered, waved handkerchiefs, and sobbed, knowing that Susan would no longer be their leader. But Susan had no plans to retire completely. She would remain an active member of the organization for the rest of her life.

The death of Susan's friend Elizabeth in 1902 served as another reminder that time was slipping away. After hearing the news, Susan sat alone in her study for several hours, until reporters pounded on the door. They asked Susan how she felt. "I am too crushed to speak," she replied. One newspaper headline read: "Anthony Left Behind." Indeed, Susan felt as if she had been left behind. Still, she continued to make herself useful.

In May of 1904, Susan headed to Berlin, Germany, for a meeting of the International Council of Women. She was thrilled that women from all over the world would once again meet to discuss women's issues. Some of the women were not happy that reporters arrived to cover the convention. But Susan said, "Welcome all reporters who want to come, the more, the better." One Berlin newspaper reported, "The Americans call her 'Aunt Susan.' She is our 'Aunt Susan' too."

At age eighty-five, Susan decided to make a return trip to the West Coast. In June of 1905, she and her sister Mary and one hundred other women traveled by train to Portland, Oregon, for a NAWSA convention. Crowds gathered at railroad stations along the way to greet them. Susan stood on the back platform, waving her handkerchief, shaking hands, and sometimes delivering a speech. While she was in Oregon, Susan unveiled a statue of Sacagawea, the Native American woman who served as a guide to explorers Lewis and Clark. Susan begged the men of Oregon to vote for women's suffrage.

In January 1906, Susan made plans to attend another NAWSA meeting, this time in Baltimore, Maryland. A blizzard hit Rochester as she left for the train station. Susan made it to Baltimore, but she caught a cold and spent most of the convention in bed. On February 15, her eighty-sixth birthday, she rode the train from Baltimore to Washington, D.C. There, friends had arranged a special birthday celebration for her. President Theodore Roosevelt sent his warmest wishes, but Susan was not impressed. She said, "I would rather have him say a word in Congress in favor of amending the Constitution to give women suffrage than to praise me endlessly." At the end of the evening, Susan stood and praised the women sitting around her. With people so devoted to women's rights, she said, "Failure is impossible."

Susan returned home weak and exhausted, with pneumonia in both lungs. She drifted in and out of consciousness. In her waking moments, she spoke the names of the women with whom she had worked. On March 13, 1906, Susan died.

Ten thousand people attended Susan's funeral at Central Presbyterian Church, in Rochester, New York. Editorials in over a thousand newspapers praised Susan. Even the *New York Times,* which had for years opposed women's suffrage, spoke of "the tender, womanly loveliness of the great reformer."

Susan's crusade did not end with her death. In towns and cities across the nation, women gathered to honor their hero. Women spoke out who had never spoken before. NAWSA membership grew from 12,000 in 1906 to over 117,000 in 1910.

In 1910, women in the state of Washington won the right to vote. California granted women voting rights in 1911. Arizona, Oregon, and Kansas followed in 1912. And finally, on August 26, 1920, President Woodrow Wilson signed into law the Nineteenth Amendment. This amendment—often called the Anthony Amendment—gave women throughout the United States the right to vote.

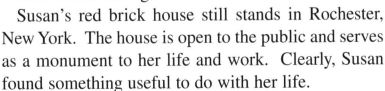

Susan's red brick house still stands in Rochester, New York. The house is open to the public and serves as a monument to her life and work. Clearly, Susan found something useful to do with her life.

Bibliography

Barry, Kathleen. *Susan B. Anthony: A Biography of a Singular Feminist.* New York: New York University Press, 1988.

Harper, Ida Husted. *The Life and Work of Susan B. Anthony.* Indianapolis: Bowen-Merrill, 1898.

Harper, Ida Husted, and Susan B. Anthony. *History of Woman Suffrage.* Vol. 4. Rochester, NY: Susan B. Anthony, 1903.

Lutz, Alma. *Susan B. Anthony: Rebel, Crusader, Humanitarian.* Boston: Beacon Press, 1959.

Stanton, Elizabeth Cady, Susan B. Anthony, and Matilda Joslyn Gage, eds. *History of Woman Suffrage.* Vol. 1. New York: Fowler & Wells Publishers, 1881.

———— *History of Woman Suffrage.* Vol. 2–3. Rochester, NY: 1882–1886.

Ward, Geoffrey C. *Not for Ourselves Alone: The Story of Elizabeth Cady Stanton and Susan B. Anthony.* New York: Knopf, 1999.

Index